The Real Estate Warrior

Volume 1
Leadership & Success

J.E. Hanley PhD (abd), MBA

Introduction

The writings of the Real Estate Warrior come from my experience over 2 decades in leadership roles. I have spent the better part of 25 years being employed, working for others, as well as operating my own businesses. I have had successes and failures – each time learning more about myself and about leadership.

My goal for this book is fairly simple – I want anyone with a desire to succeed to have the opportunity to learn about effective and powerful leadership in a way that is entertaining and thought provoking.

It is my sincere desire that the writings are enjoyable and provides each reader something special that they can take with them in all they do in business and in life.

I dedicate this book to my family who have always been an inspiration and have taught me more than they can ever realize.

Enjoy!!

The Real Estate Warrior

Volume 1

Leadership & Success

Chapters

Chapter 1
Becoming the Real Estate Warrior
– Slave No More

In today's society the idea of a warrior is pretty much removed from the ordinary person's vocabulary. There is no need for hunters and gatherers, fighting over scarce resources in a "dog-eat-dog" world. Really? In today's society of Internet and Amazon purchases, Uber pickups, and fast convenient dinners that provide instantaneous gratification it's no wonder that today's home buyers and sellers want it NOW!!!

Being a warrior in the real estate industry is about knowing your clients, their hopes, their dreams, and their aspirations – whether they are selling a home or buying a home. Whether it is for the first time or the 10th time, or whether or not they are dual buyer/seller...the importance of knowing your client better than ever is the key to being a Real

Estate Warrior. Likewise it is vital that the client know their Real Estate Warrior. It is important to know your real estate agent's educational background and their experience in negotiating, applying sale techniques, and their level of aggressiveness or lack thereof in pursuing your desired home as well as your stated outcome.

This concept of YOUR CLIENTS often escapes the home buyer and seller. Often times the real estate industry in its quest to make sure the real estate agent is perceived as "the expert" and that regular folks could not complete a real estate transaction on their own have foregone the concept of YOUR CLIENTS. This is a fairly easy and straight forward concept – those individuals that are buying homes are the clients of those selling homes and vice versa. Therefore, home sellers and their agents must work in collaboration with each other to attract the ready, willing and able home buyers. Conversely, home buyers and their agents must diligently seek and search for the home that will satisfy all or most of their home buying needs.

In most cases the real estate agent becomes the de facto "buyer" or "owner" of a property whether they want the title and responsibility or not. The Real Estate Warrior understands that the battle is afoot the moment the real estate "For Sale" sign is staked into the property's ground. The concept of a warrior – one who shows great vigor, courage or aggressiveness – is a concept often associated with athletes or social causes not necessarily with real estate. But, Real Estate Warriors do exist – they are the type of agents that hunt the landscape and fight for their clients – buyers and sellers just need to look for them. The Real Estate Warrior is one who will work on the buyer or seller's behalf tirelessly to "fleece" your opponent and garner you the best deal possible – whether you are buying or selling a home.

What does it mean to be a slave? A slave to what? In the past the slave was beholden to a master. In today's society that master is debt!! The more debt you have the more you must work to free yourself. In order to free yourself you must make sacrifices – a cheaper automobile, a smaller home, skip a vacation or forego something of pleasure that appeals to you. The larger the debt load the more sacrifices need to be made. Debt is the master, you are the slave. Where does debt come from? One of the leading factors of debt comes from education. The old formula for success included attending a college or trade school, spending tens of thousands of dollars to "get an education". This education was your key to success. The price of education was considered "good debt" since it would bring you employment that allowed you to make a good living and pay back your "good debt". According to www.studentloanhero.com[1], the average individual in 2017 carries $37,172 in student loan debt and overall it's a 1.45 trillion dollar industry!!! (That's

$1,450,000,000!!!). There are 44.2 million people carrying student loan debt, making a monthly payment of $200 to $351 per month. This debt impacts the ability of buyers to purchase other items and maintain credit. Those "other items" include buying a home.

Other kinds of debt also limit the freedom for people to use their money the way they wish. Credit card debt is another factor that binds people in the chains of debt. According to www.creditcard.com, LLC[2], today 43% of Baby Boomers carry credit card balances. Is debt normal? Today's society teaches us that debt is normal. We are raised to believe that the only way to go on to higher education is with student loans, that everyone uses and needs credit cards and that debt is a normal part of life. But is it really? Does it have to be?

It is imperative to the success of home buyers and home sellers to have a Real Estate Warrior who understands how debt has affected society and the housing market. Understanding that most buyers carry debt and that debt can affect their ability to purchase a home is one of the very first discussions to have with your client. Having a good mortgage broker/lender as part of your Warrior Team is critical to helping others succeed. This lender needs to be knowledgeable about the local market; the national trends in mortgages and can offer options that best fit your client.

The skills of the Real Estate Warrior are a set that has been honed through many battles and successfully completed transactions. The skill set is sharp and reinforced through continued education and understanding the real estate market trends – both nationally and locally – AND applying that knowledge to each clients' particular needs. The Real Estate Warrior develops the communication array that satisfies the client, and keeps the client informed of the activity or lack of activity happening particular to their needs.

If the Real Estate Warrior is working for the client selling property then the communication addresses the client's need for information about activity on the home – how many agents and potential buyers are viewing the home, how many websites the home is featured on and what is the traffic like, how does the price of the home compare with other competitor homes and is the condition of the home impeding its sale. The Real Estate Warrior is able to answer their client's questions, allay their concerns and fears and focus positive energy towards the ultimate goal – the sale of the home for the most amount of money in the shortest amount of time for the selling client.

If the Real Estate Warrior is working for the client buying a home then the communication revolves around the client's specific needs and wants for a particular home – style of home (ranch style, 2 story, etc), number of bedrooms, number of bathrooms, with or without a garage, a small/large yard, and location. The Real Estate Warrior keeps focus on the market and provides the client with new opportunities to view homes and keeps abreast of all new homes coming on the market. This is essential for the buying client to be successful in finding their new home.

The Real Estate Warrior is a rare breed these days – there seems to be a trend toward real estate agents wanting LESS contact with their clients. The idea that a perfect transaction would be to complete a transaction without ever meeting the client seems prevalent in today's industry. This notion and attitude continues to negatively impact industry confidence and subverts the very reason for the existence of the real estate agent. Looking for and finding the Real Estate Warrior can be difficult, especially when buyers and sellers end up choosing the first real estate agent they meet.

NOT ALL AGENTS ARE THE SAME AND LENGTH OF TIME AS A REAL ESTATE AGENT DOES NOT TRANSLATE INTO A SUCCESSFUL AGENT

The first truism in real estate – there are agents that have been agents for 10, 20, 30 even 40 years. The current average age for a real estate agent entering the industry is 53 years old!!! The current average age of a real estate broker is even older!!! Not all agents / brokers are the same. The number of Real Estate Warriors are even less!!! It becomes the first responsibility of the buyer and/or seller to make a wise and informed decision when deciding on the agent they will use – it should not be the agent you know but the agent who knows the market and possesses the skill set needed to meet the needs of a buying or selling client.

Another aspect of the Real Estate Warrior's arsenal of weapons to be used to fight the good fight on behalf of the client is the continued proliferation of technology and uses of the Internet. Prior to the Internet the real estate agent had "the book" – not really a book, more of a binder that held the "secret" data and information that home buyers and sellers needed or wanted. Although to be fair most buyers and sellers had no clue what they needed. The binder contained physical hard copy paper sheets of current (or as current as could be given the agent) inventory of the agent's own listings as well as the other agents. The binder would be updated by calling or going to the real estate office – i.e. running all over town – to get the most up to date data. The updates would be new listings, pending sales and sold homes. So every week a lot of time and energy was directed at updating "the book" which made "the book" a valuable weapon (and in some cases the only weapon) an agent had going into battle.

This notion of "the book" serves as a great example of one of the most important – if not the most important – aspect of a real estate agent's ability and success – and that is TIME. I have heard "You can always make more money, but you can't make more time"...this adage is oh so true in real estate.

REAL ESTATE IS A ZERO SUM GAME

The notion of time is extremely important to the Real Estate Warrior - time is the one commodity that all agents have – we all have the same 24 hours in a day – the key for the Real Estate Warrior is what productivity is accomplished versus the activity that is done by the Warrior. The notion of Zero Sum Game is fairly straight forward:

If I Win, You Lose.
If You Win, I Lose.

DO NOT CONFUSE ACTIVITY WITH ACCOMPLISHMENT

(Sorry for the digression - So the proliferation of technology and use of the Internet)

So prior to the Internet the agent's best weapon was "the book" – which represented one thing the agent had the buyer or seller did not have which was *ACCESS* to information pertinent to particular homes in the market. The real estate agent, like all real estate agents of the time, was selling access to information that buyers and sellers wanted AND the only way to get access to the magical "book" of information was through the real estate agent. So, did Real Estate Warriors exist in the past?

Real Estate Warriors have always been present in every market during every time period since the advent of the first real estate office in 1851.

The Real Estate Warrior is the agent who knew that there was more to the market than just what appeared to be the market. The Real Estate Warrior sees beyond the current conditions, understands the nuances of subtle (and not subtle shifts) in market conditions and hones their skill set constantly and methodically so that they are top producers regardless of the market conditions. At the forefront of every Real Estate Warrior are the needs of the client and building a positive long lasting relationship with them. Understanding this concept is critical to the Real Estate Warriors success.

ACCESS TO INFORMATION SHOULD NOT BE CONFOUNDED BY MAN-MADE OBSTACLES

The prior business model of real estate was a business that monetizes the knowledge and information available NOT how that knowledge and information was utilized for the betterment of the client. The Internet turned that model upside down and created a model in which HOW information was used became more important than the information itself – since everyone now had access to "the book". This is the critical difference between a real estate agent and a Real Estate Warrior. The Warrior understands that information restricted will always be released in some form or fashion for free or fee and that the "demand" can be monetized in other ways. Certainly for the Real Estate Warrior that way is through relationship building activities, meeting client needs and wants and building trust so when the time comes the buyer and/or seller will know that (1) they have a Real Estate Warrior and not just a real estate agent and (2) in their heart that their Real Estate Warrior is working on their behalf and in **their best interest**.

So the Real Estate Warrior is selling "know how" of the information, selling trust and selling expertise. It has been said that there are over 100 steps to completing a real estate transaction and without the expertise of a real estate agent the buyer and/or seller could miss something or get something wrong that could cost money or the sale itself.

YOU NEED A REAL ESTATE AGENT!!!

Really?? Is this statement true? In the history of real estate ALL successful transactions had at least one real estate agent attached to it? Obviously the answer is that real estate transactions can and do reach a successful closing with and without real estate agents. The focus should be the transaction process and how the experience is for the buyer and the seller. The Real Estate Warrior understands this focus and delights in the ability to make sure the transaction moves forward as stress free as possible for their client.

For the remainder of this book, I will help to process what this complex and intriguing business of real estate actually holds for the future of agents, clients and society in general. The changes that are occurring in this industry at the end of 2017 is mind bending – everything from Redfin to Block Chain and digital currency – and the Real Estate Warrior will continue to play a critical and vital role in assisting clients. One thing is certain – the buying and selling of property is NOT stopping and will always be woven into the fabric of our society – socially, economically, and most of all personally.

Come take the ride.

Learn some things new.

Become a more informed consumer and agent so that the real estate industry grows and thrives –

. . . . It is, after all, all of our responsibility!!!

Chapter 2

Real Estate Warrior – Why You Need One

The Internet

Does the Internet spell the end of the real estate agent? After all, other professions have succumbed to the World Wide Web – travel agents, encyclopedia salesmen, music stores, financial advisors, Blockbuster – all these professions having to change their focus or reinvent their expertise and knowledge in order to survive and thrive (or not survive) in this new world order of the Internet. Nowadays, consumers have been seduced by instant gratification of online delivery of information, streaming entertainment and the ability to get essentials (food, drink, transportation) at the click of a button and onward through the hierarchy of needs and become self actualized – all through the Internet. In an age where interaction with another person may actually hinder your ability to complete a task; many are avoiding the hassle and just doing it themselves.

As a Real Estate Warrior this must be a recognized and accepted factor in building relationships – sometimes people just want left alone!! Wait. What? Real estate has long been built on the notion that we must provide our time and expertise to the unsuspecting and un-informed public. There it is again – the notion of time. It's important that the Real Estate Warrior understand that it's not just their time being used but it is also their client's time that is being used. This notion is often lost on the real estate agent; however the Real Estate Warrior takes pride in respecting their client's time as well as their own.

I WILL TELL YOU WHEN YOU ARE WASTING MY TIME

The Real Estate Warrior is built for the long haul – developing and cultivating their client's trust and having a relationship that is mutually beneficial for both parties. As with any healthy relationship there must be boundaries that are enforced and respected by the parties involved. The Real Estate Warrior understands this and begins to establish these boundaries for the sake of the relationship at the very first contact with the potential client. Notice I said potential client – at the first contact that is what the home buyer or seller is. In a business that never utters this phrase aloud, it is the Real Estate Warrior that decides who they work with and who they do not work with!!!

Most real estate agents will work with anybody – and I mean anybody –in the short term. The short term is defined as showing the prospective buyer a couple of homes before they have any type of mortgage pre-approval from a respectable lender. The real estate agent justifies the use of this time since they are "building rapport" and "establishing a relationship" with the buyer without pressuring the buyer or scaring them away. I call BULLSHIT!!! The real estate agent knows that if they do not work with this buyer then another agent will – remember it's a ZERO SUM GAME – and they are willing to risk their most precious commodity (whether they know it or not) and spend time with someone who may or may not be able to buy a home.

It is only after some time has been expended that the real estate agent finds out if the buyer is ready, willing and able to purchase a home. This is the time period that most Real Estate Warriors NEVER encounter!!! The Real Estate Warrior – out of respect for the profession, their time and their client's time – will make sure that the buyer is ready, willing and able to purchase a home BEFORE showing them ANY home.

The Real Estate Warrior cultivates relationships from the start – at the very first contact and begins forging a positive long lasting relationship. Wait. What? Conventional wisdom in real estate says if you push too hard the client will go to another agent – after all, currently there are 1,300,000 REALTORS in the United States - the most since 2007-2008 (when the bubble burst)! Conventional wisdom says that agents need to take cues from their clients and allow the client to dictate the process and if you don't the client will go elsewhere. If you make the client mad the client will go elsewhere. If the client does not like what you tell them – even if it is accurate and true – the client will go to someone else. You will lose the sale and not get a commission and not earn a living and not be able to be successful – again – I call BULLSHIT!!!

Ok, now that we have explored the myths and fallacies that permeate the business environment and the teachings of an apparent old business model – let us discuss WHY you need to be a Real Estate Warrior and WHY your clients need a Real Estate Warrior. Noticed I said a Real Estate Warrior NOT a real estate agent.

A real estate agent, in the eye of the buyer or seller, is nothing short of a necessary evil. If they had the confidence to go it alone – they would. At the very first contact every real estate professional is a real estate agent to that buyer and seller. What happens during the initial interaction helps the buyer and seller recognize the Real Estate Warrior – if you are one. The client determines who, what, when and how the process will proceed.

THE CLIENT IS IN CONTROL

This is a difficult concept – not to understand but to accept – for many a real estate agent. How can the client be in control? We are the ones with the expertise and skill – aren't we? Maybe so, but the client has access to information (remember "the book") instantaneously thanks to the World Wide Web. If the client does not trust you – nothing you say or do will move that relationship further. In fact, when clients enter the realm of a real estate agent and then disappear after one or two showings and they don't return emails and the professional is fighting to maintain contact with them (i.e. your conversion rate from prospect to client) for the ones that are lost – IT'S NOT THE CLIENT'S FAULT.

Today's client is not forced to meet with an agent. The ability of the Real Estate Warrior to use their skill set to build a positive long lasting relationship does not "make" the client do anything, but does encourage the client to recognize what is in their (the client) own best interest and "WANT" to work with their Real Estate Warrior. The concept of "want" is critical to building the positive long lasting relationship – because clients who want to do something are more likely to understand WHY it is important to their success. Understanding the client's wants is just as important as gaining the client's trust – in fact, understanding their wants will increase the trust they have in their Real Estate Warrior.

So, given the environment and the power of the Internet the question that begs to be answered is simply "Why do I need a Real Estate Agent /Warrior?" The answer to that question lies within the profession itself. Real estate, like any other business, relies on the ability to present itself as having individuals that can know things and do things that other cannot do for themselves...or will not do for themselves. There is a notion in real estate that equates gaining additional knowledge assists in earning higher income and is echoed throughout the real estate industry. The notion that the more education you receive about real estate "stuff" the more money you will make because you will be better able to serve your clients, the better you serve your clients the better your reputation will be and the better your reputation the more clients will want to use your services. It sounds fairly simple and straight forward doesn't it? This is an example of the structural foundations of an industry that attempts to set its members apart from the rest of the general public. Real estate is designed to be a foreign concept with its own culture, language, ethics and principles – it is the basis as to why the "expert" is needed to guide the unsuspecting client through the mazes, jungles and pitfalls of the real estate transaction and bring them safely to the closing oasis so that the client may revel in the glory of their sale or purchase ....Wait. What?

This notion of exclusivity builds value. But it is quality of that value that becomes important – would you purchase a diamond at full price that had a flaw in its caret, clarity, color or cut? Probably not!! But in real estate there are lots of agents with significant flaws that get business every day. These agents do the bare minimum, have poor communication, worse yet may not know the laws and regulations and have very little command over the procedures of a transaction because they only do a hand full of transactions in a year. In other words, clients are paying for a real estate tourist or hobbyist NOT a real estate agent and certainly NOT a Real Estate Warrior.

NOT ALL AGENTS ARE THE SAME AND LENGTH OF TIME AS A REAL ESTATE AGENT DOES NOT MEAN THAT THE AGENT IS SUCCESSFUL

The Real Estate Warrior brings professionalism, knowledge, expertise as well as warmth, thoughtfulness, friendship and kindness to every relationship that is cultivated. The client is enveloped in a trusting embrace that makes the client feel safe, wanted and acknowledged throughout and after the transaction is concluded. The reason why the client needs a Real Estate Warrior in their corner is to experience real estate at its apex – the vision comes to life through the actions and concerted efforts of you, the Real Estate Warrior.

The old adage "You get what you pay for" has never been truer than in real estate. Most people don't have a crystal ball and cannot predict the future. Those that do seem to remain fairly quiet or are too busy predicting the end of the world. A lot of folks worry about the uncertainty of the future and do their best to control what will happen. In real estate, as in life, there are few certainties and the Real Estate Warrior is there to help manage client's questions, anxieties and concerns so that clients can make well informed decisions. Having a Real Estate Warrior or just a real estate agent can make a world of difference in the process of the transaction and a successful outcome of the real estate transaction.

Chapter 3
The Warrior Formula

Building a successful anything requires a couple of items in the tool box. The items that are needed to become a successful Real Estate Warrior have been explored and developed over a period of time and through many real estate experiences – some great, some good and some just plain awful. It has been through a collective experience in which the openness to the experience itself is vital to learning about the Real Estate Warrior. Wait. What?

What you just read sounds like some Zen-like, mystic, new-age mantra about self-enlightenment. It doesn't make it any less true. Part of becoming a Real Estate Warrior is the experience of actively working in the real estate business. Being a Real Estate Warrior starts with thinking like a Real Estate Warrior. We will get to this in a little while. Right now the important thing to recognize is that every real estate agent has the ability to choose to be a Real Estate Warrior. Just like everyone has the same 24 hours in a day, what becomes important is how that time is used.

DO NOT CONFUSE ACTIVITY WITH ACCOMPLISHMENT

Becoming a Real Estate Warrior is a process and starts with the proper mindset. This leads into the development of the proper skill set that creates opportunities to employ strategies at the right time in the right circumstances while hearing and listening to your client's needs and wants and adapting and overcoming any barriers to meeting those needs and wants. Sounds like a great deal of time and energy? It is. Yeah, but is it worth it? That's up to the real estate agent – remember we all have the same amount of time; the difference is how we use it and how productive we are with the time we have available.

Today's real estate industry seems to be driven by technology – Internet websites promoting For Sale By Owner (FSBO) sites that allow sellers to forego the expertise of a real estate professional and thus, save money. Sites that promote "peer-to-peer" buying and selling; and with the advent of Block Chain technology it may be possible in the near future for real estate transactions to be completed within minutes/hours/days instead of weeks and months. The industry does not favor "it's the way we have always done it" mentality and provides opportunity after opportunity to enhance the insight and actions of the Real Estate Warrior.

EXPERTISE CAN BE ENHANCED BY, NOT REPLACED BY, TECHNOLOGY

The expertise possessed by the Real Estate Warrior can be enhanced by technology but technology will not replace the Real Estate Warrior. Buying and selling a home – at its core – is a very *personal and financial transaction*. In life, most people hold close to their heart 2 things – their family and their finances. The financial transaction of buying and selling a home has been said to be one of the most important decisions you will make in your lifetime. Wow – what a statement!!! No wonder it can be such a nerve racking experience.

Think about it - will an individual or couple ever make a more important decision? It's a decision that could cost for the next 30 years of a person's life!!! Because it is such an important decision the need to have wisdom in making that decision is priceless. The more wisdom you have the more informed your decision will be. Where does the wisdom come from? Wisdom is defined as "knowledge of what is true or right coupled with the just judgment as to action"[3]

The second factor in the successfulness of a real estate transaction is trust. Trust that you are making a sound decision, trust that the home is right for your needs and wants, trust that the transaction will conclude favorably, trust that you are getting the very best deal you can. That's a lot of trust!!! Trust comes from the development of a positive long lasting relationship that has been built on consistent, reliable and accurate actions that strengthen faith and belief in each other. The level of trust is equal to the level of confidence placed in a person to be beneficial to another. In other words, trust comes from the Real Estate Warrior and client acting in a manner that demonstrates an understanding of each other's needs and wants and actions that promote a positive outcome for both parties.

WISDOM & TRUST ARE PRICELESS

As the future of real estate and technology continue to intersect with the clients that are buying and/or selling homes will continue to demand a level of professionalism, knowledge and expertise from those in the profession. The Real Estate Warrior can thrive in this environment. Make no mistake – there are no good shortcuts to becoming a Real Estate Warrior. The process and development is a personal decision and one that dictates the future of each agent. The formula for the Real Estate Warrior does not have to be complex but it does need to be thoughtful. The ability of understanding the needs and wants of others, placing their needs ahead of your own, being rigorously honest and faithful to your client (even if being honest means making them angry) and always looking after the best interest of your client. These are the hallmarks of a successful Real Estate Warrior.

Chapter 4
Real Estate Warrior Relationship Building

As long as human interaction is required for a successful real estate transaction the ability to build a positive long lasting relationship will be paramount to the level of success achieved in the real estate industry. There are no computer programs or algorithms that can replace the feel of a trusted handshake. At the core of it, buying or selling a home is a very personal and financial transaction. The needs and wants of each person involved must be accounted for if the transaction is to be successful.

As Spyro Kemble from Inman states "Building relationships requires going beyond the annual holiday gift bag and the occasional "Hello"[4]. The Real Estate Warrior must learn how to foster rapport, and more importantly – trust". Typically we learn lessons throughout our lives and take those lessons and incorporate them into our world view and actions. We use this world view to deal with the universe around us. This also includes how we interact with other people. Building relationships and creating trust takes skill and honesty. So, what is the best way to build those positive, long lasting relationships with clients?

The amount of research, studies and literature on building healthy relationships, building strong relationships, relationships with your spouse, your children, other people, co-workers, your bosses, and your employees goes on and on. It is vast and fills millions of pages on the Internet and in books. The ability to understand the importance of relationship building is the starting point.

UNDERSTAND THE "WHY" AND YOU WILL BE ABLE TO DEVELOP THE "HOW"

So, let's start with the "Why". Why put forth a lot of time and energy to build positive long lasting relationships with people who, realistically, are usually only in your sphere for a short period of time. Let's really think about this. The normal process of buying/selling a home once a buyer has made an offer and a seller has accepted that offer – the time of the relationship, albeit a very intense relationship, is approximately 45 to 60 days. Once the transaction is concluded the buyers have received what they wanted (A home), the sellers have received what they wanted (Their home sold), the real estate professionals have received what they wanted (Paid) and everyone goes back to their busy lives and moves forward. Why then, is the Real Estate Warrior at all concerned about building a positive long lasting relationship after the deal is concluded?

In every relationship there are factors that determine the type of relationship you have. We have all kinds of relationships – from serious and intense to casual relationships. You have relationships that you have chosen to have and others that have been forced upon you, such as:

Thrust Upon You	Choice You Make
Father / Mother	Friends
Siblings	Significant Other
Teachers	Children
Bosses / Co-Workers	Pets

As you grow these relationships change and have either more or less significance in your life and sphere of influence. One thing is certain you are either cultivating a relationship or you are not. You are either strengthening relationships or you are not. Either way it is you making the decision.

IF YOU THINK YOU CAN OR THINK YOU CAN'T – YOU ARE RIGHT

So how does the Real Estate Warrior take on relationship building, where does the Warrior's time and energy get focused? When building positive, long lasting relationships – both personal and professional relationships - the Real Estate Warrior adheres to six principles to make the most and get the most out of relationships:

Warrior Principle #1 – Think of Others

The Real Estate Warrior spends every day making sure that relationships are cultivated by thinking about others and putting into action and deed to demonstrate that thoughtfulness. Real estate giant Brian Buffini calls it the "Unexpected Extras"[5]. The Warrior takes time to let someone know they are special and through action strengthens and improves the relationship.

Warrior Principle #2 – Take Responsibility

Real estate can be a brutal business...often times tensions can run very high as we are dealing with one of the most important transactions of a person's lifetime. There can be times when the transaction stalls, runs into a barrier and it is the Real Estate Warrior, in the stressful times, who steps to the plate. Taking responsibility is the cornerstone of great relationships. Taking responsibility and not laying blame elsewhere shows courage. The courage to not let uncomfortable discussions be delayed and the stressful times continue and fester, the Real Estate Warrior finds a solution and moves the relationship (and the transaction) forward.

Warrior Principle #3 – On a Consistent Basis – Give

The Real Estate Warrior recognizes great relationships are ones that provide mutual benefit to both parties. The Warrior cultivates relationships through the sharing of information, helping others understand the connections being made and always thinking about the wants and needs of the other person.

Warrior Principle #4 – Valuing the Relationship & Staying Visible

The Real Estate Warrior understands the value of relationships and approaches relationships with a "Power With" rather than "Power Over" way of thinking. This means that the relationship is a team and works **together** to be successful. The Real Estate Warrior may discount the message but NEVER discounts the messenger. Staying visible is a top "to do" for the Real Estate Warrior. For the Warrior staying visible to their clients is the channel for providing valuable up to date information about the market – whether they are buyer clients or seller clients or both. Providing information AND understanding the client's motivation keeps the Real Estate Warrior relevant to their clients and builds trust in creating the positive, long lasting relationships.

Warrior Principle #5 – Anticipate the Need

The Real Estate Warrior anticipates the needs of their clients, of their spouses, their friends or their children. The need for awareness beyond ourselves is how the Real Estate Warrior does this. The Real Estate Warrior understands that the questions that are not asked can be the most important to answer. Understanding the ability to help others reach their goals will build long lasting success.

Warrior Principle #6 – Know When to Let Go

The Real Estate Warrior understands that sometimes the only thing to do is to end a relationship that is toxic, that is draining and that does not produce positive outcomes. In real estate often times relationships are started out of convenience – the buyer or seller make contact with a real estate agent and off they go looking at houses, getting a market analysis and doing all the things that involves a real estate agent. Often times it can feel like a lopsided one-way relationship with the agent putting in the majority of the time and effort.

The Real Estate Warrior works to build a positive, long lasting relationship based on mutual needs and wants that will have a beneficial outcome for both parties – it doesn't always happen. The Real Estate Warrior is not afraid to move on from relationships when necessary – knowing that their business will continue to prosper and thrive.

The idea of building positive, long lasting relationships is a linchpin to having a successful real estate business. The relationships that get formed and cultivated are the relationships that allow for referrals, repeat business and word of mouth marketing, which can translate into more opportunities to build new relationships. This relationship building cycle relies on the Real Estate Warrior understanding and abilities. These abilities must be honed, exercised daily and nurtured if they are to produce positive results. Each day is the opportunity to either build a positive long lasting relationship or not --- but as always, it's your choice.

Re-Cap

So, before we proceed, it's time for a short Recap of what we have learned. This will help understand where we are at and where we are going. These concepts will help provide you with a level of understanding of the Real Estate Warrior thus far...

1. **The importance of knowing your client better than ever is the key to being a Real Estate Warrior**

2. **Home sellers and their agents must work in collaboration with each other to attract the ready, willing and able home buyers. Conversely, home buyers and their agents must diligently seek and search for the home that will satisfy all or most of their home buying needs**

3. **Looking for and finding the Real Estate Warrior can be difficult, especially when you go with the first real estate agent you meet**

4. **Real Estate is a ZERO SUM GAME**

5. **Not all agents are the same and length of time as a real estate agent does not mean that the agent is a successful agent**

6. **Don't Confuse Activity with Accomplishment**

7. **Technology can enhance not replace the real estate agent**

8. **Wisdom and Truth are Priceless**

9. **Understand the "Why" and you will be able to develop the "How"**

Warrior Principles can help cultivate positive, long lasting relationships and the Real Estate Warrior is not afraid to lose relationships when they are unproductive.

Chapter 5
The Real Estate Industry –
Truth & Consequences

So let's talk about real estate as a business. What does it take to build a successful real estate business? This question is a "simply complex" question with an answer that might surprise you!!

BEING A REAL ESTATE AGENT IS EASY BEING A SUCCESSFUL REAL ESTATE AGENT IS NOT

There are close to 2 million real estate agents and REALTORS® working in over 86,000 Brokerages in the United States, as of 2012[6]. As you are reading this those 2 million individuals are trying to be successful with their real estate business. Some will succeed and others (many others) will fail. The industry has changed in the past 10 years – since the dark times of the housing bubble and subsequent crash. In the past decade homes prices have risen back to pre-crash levels, although inventory of homes continues to lag behind. Interest rates, which have remained under 3.99% for the longest time, are now creeping over 4.00% as we head into 2018. The US economy continues to improve and our Gross Domestic Product (GPD – measures economic strength) will increase by 2.7% at the end of 2017[7]. We live in interesting times and, as a real estate agent, have chosen an interesting way to make a living.

How does a real estate agent get paid? Do they get paid for showing the house? For listing the home? Do they get paid every 2 weeks like a "normal" job? The answer my friend is NO. The real estate agent and the Brokerage firm only make money when a home is sold and the title/deed is transferred to a new owner. The selling process can take as little as 15 days or as long as "forever" – it all depends. One of the greatest phrases in the business world is "It all depends". This phrase encapsulates the real estate transaction.

You see, dear reader, real estate is not for the faint of heart – It requires a Real Estate Warrior mentality. Before we get into the nitty gritty of the real estate transaction I would like to spend a little bit of time addressing the "make up" of the real estate agent.

WHO IN THEIR RIGHT MIND WOULD WANT TO MAKE THIS THEIR PROFESSION?

Today's real estate agent is an average age of 53 years old[8]. This is the average, which means there are agents in their "golden years" still actively practicing their profession and there are 18 to 25 year olds just starting their career. How in the world can we build positive long lasting relationships with everyone from the age of 18 to 70 and beyond when each requires different skill sets, communication abilities and language differences. By language differences I mean that the way someone speaks and the words they use may be somewhat different if you are 21 versus someone who is 65 years old. The industry, at any given time, has different generations serving the same profession and working toward a similar goal of securing clients who are ready, willing and able to buy and sell homes.

The idea of having the time to cultivate relationships and build positive long lasting relationships almost seems impossible for the real estate agent who already has so much on their plate. Professionally, showing homes, listing homes, writing up contracts, following up with clients, marketing to and prospecting new clients and following up on leads, negotiating deals, reading home inspection reports, preparing clients for closings, contacting lenders and closing companies and insurance agents and scheduling and conducting final walk through, etc, etc, etc....remembering over 100 steps from start to finish for a real estate transaction. That's just a real estate agents professional life. We haven't even delved into their personal life!!! It's easy to be a real estate agent but it's hard to be a successful real estate agent. Creating the necessary work-life balance that everyone speaks of is elusive at times.

<u>BEING A REAL ESTATE AGENT IS EASY BEING A SUCCESSFUL REAL ESTATE AGENT IS NOT</u>

So why do people fail at being a successful real estate agent? Why do some thrive year after year and others falter and consistently miss opportunities. Mindset, attitude, state of mind – whatever you label it – it is the one thing that seems to set apart successful agents from non-successful agents. How you approach your real estate business

– yes it is a business – is the foundation and cornerstone – so, the question that needs asked consistently is the foundation of your business solid? Is it shaky? Does it even exist? Building the proper attitude toward your business is key to success.

So build your real estate foundation for the long haul – one that is built to last!!!

Many real estate agents get into real estate with very little experience in sales / commission-only environment and are ill prepared for the joys of not being paid for 45 to 60 days after an accepted deal, and that assumes nothing falls apart during that time. Above the monetary aspect is another important aspect that is more internal to the real estate agent. In a world in which we hear the word "No" twenty five times more often than we hear the word "Yes" the development of strong internal sense is vital because "No" can be your motivator or your defeater. Real Estate – as an industry – does not care how many times you are told "No", it does not care if you make zero sales in a month. The structure of the industry allows the individual to make what they make of it – it provides the opportunities - whether the agent wants it or not.

One of the separations that occur for successful real estate agents is the development of a business wide system that addresses the key points of their business plan and practices. The "system" has been addressed by a multitude of others eager to take your money in return for a canned program that will help you prospect, generate leads, convert leads and help "your business grow". They all offer similar packages with added twists to set them apart. The point is this - the need to have a "system" that allows you to consistently meet the needs of your clients, keep you visible to your clients and new clients and provide the means to maintain productive levels of accomplishments (i.e. sales) is critical to success. The work is the work – all agents are trying to reach the same goal which is to sell homes and properties. In this Zero Sum Game called real estate you either win or lose.

The downward spiral of a busted deal!!! Ever have a situation in which you attempted to accomplish something, put together a plan, gather support for that plan, executed that plan at the right time only to have something happen to thwart your success. Whenever a deal goes south it creates very intense feelings of failure, anger, sorrow and any other negative emotion you want to throw in. Agents have lost clients over transactions that ended prior to a successful closing.

These situations can define a real estate agent – but only if the agent allows it. The Real Estate Warrior NEVER allows a broken deal to be the end of their business. In fact, the broken deal is an opportunity to learn something new, whether that "new thing" is about your client, the other agent or yourself. The Real Estate Warrior understands that deals end prior to a successful closing, that people's emotions can run high and building and maintaining positive, long lasting relationships can be tested.

THE "DRAMA OF REAL ESTATE" WILL LEAVE YOU LESS THAN WHAT YOU STARTED WITH

What happens when that client you have been working with suddenly falls off the radar, doesn't return calls or emails and no longer asking for your advice, or worse yet, is no longer interested in looking at homes with you. It almost transports you to high school days – why don't you like me anymore? What did I do wrong? It's not you; it's me – creating doubt in the agent's mind. Trying to figure what went wrong needs to be a focused exercise on the agent themselves and not on the client or other person. If real estate teaches one thing it's that you can only control yourself and not others.

We started by saying a critical aspect to a successful real estate business is attitude. That attitude being that you, the agent, makes the decision to be great at your business. Yeah, I know it sounds like a platitude, and it is, but it does not make it any less true. How many agents think real estate is a hard business full of pitfalls, negative people, liars, cheaters, cut throats and a hundred other unpleasant things beyond your control? Also, that real estate requires long hours, no vacations, interrupted dinners, TV shows and time with family and friends. These are agents that are constantly working and available to agents, clients and prospects – ALL. THE. TIME. Or you are not – it's your choice. Working 24/7 may generate a nice cash return but can that pace be maintained?

Recently there have been a lot of promotions offering work-life balance. Work less and make more money!!! Again these programs may or may not work for you as an agent. But the important factor in all this is YOU. How you think about your business is just as important of how you practice your business. The Real Estate Warrior has an empowered focus that concentrates on creating and maintaining a disciplined practice, an attitude of positive thinking and a "do what it takes" mindset. This will help recognize opportunities to succeed. In essence, building a system that allows the agent's belief in one's self and level of perseverance that creates opportunities for success.

Real estate is about competition. Competition comes in many forms – competition for clients, competition for lenders, competition for home inspectors, competition for insurance agents, competition for listing homes, etc... Everyone involved in a real estate transaction – and there is lot of people – compete everyday for business. Remember it's a Zero Sum Game – If Lender A gets your buyer's business then Lender B does not. This goes for the home inspection, the insurance agent, the moving company, and every other business that the buyer or seller could utilize.

All of these businesses compete on a daily basis – wanting buyers and sellers to know they offer the best quality, better rates, less costs, better options – whatever works to gain business. Additionally, any one of these "team members" can throw a wrench into the closing process. Having strong business practices as a foundation and systems in place bring the odds of success up exponentially.

Real Estate Transaction Team

**Buyer, Buyer Agent, Buyer Closing Agent, Seller,
Seller Agent, Seller Closing Agent,
Lender, Underwriter, Appraiser,
Home Inspector, Municipalities,
Insurance Agent, Movers**

The real estate industry offers opportunities to those that recognize those opportunities, look through the negative aspects of the business and focus on winning that Zero Sum Game. Not committing the same mistakes over and over again is also important to build a successful business. Understanding the "why" of our actions lets the agent to honestly look at and review their actions and, more importantly, their results.

The Real Estate Warrior understands that this humbling exercise can be powerful and conducts it on a routine basis. The ability to learn from mistakes allows the Real Estate Warrior to grow and become even more successful. In the real estate industry the ability to remain grounded when successful and determined when not starts with a positive attitude and remains a factor in successful businesses and is absent in ones that do not last.

Chapter 6
Transformational vs. Transactional

In the context of this book transformational refers to a long term focus, centered on building positive, long lasting relationships. Transactional refers to a short term focus, centered on the next client and next transaction. Both are important and both are used to build a successful business in the real estate industry. Transformational is about Leadership, transactional is about Management.

LEADERS DO THE RIGHT THING
MANAGERS DO THINGS RIGHT

This is not to imply that managers don't do the right thing. Being a Real Estate Warrior running a real estate business means being a manager AND being a leader, which one you are at any given moment often depends on the situation at hand. The Real Estate Warrior understands that being a leader and being a manager is part and parcel with running a real estate business. Let me say that again – to be a Real Estate Warrior you MUST be both a leader and a manager and you must play each role at the right time with the right people in the right situations.

The idea that a real estate transaction involves many people identifies the need for both leadership to assure the right thing is done (e.g. laws are followed, ethics are adhere to) and that things are done right (e.g. contracts are filled out and signed, timeframes are adhered to, communication happens, etc). With all these people involved a transaction can go very wrong very quickly. The Real Estate Warrior makes sure that the rules are understood and followed ALWAYS – not when it's beneficial, not when it's convenient – ALWAYS!!! By doing the right thing each and every time the Real Estate Warrior can concentrate on relationships. Doing business this way may cause some short term pain and anxiety (possibly losing a deal) but it builds trust and integrity.

Being a leader requires one thing – you have followers. Throughout history there have been effective leaders, there have been mediocre leaders and there have been downright awful leaders. What made the difference?

The very last thing anyone wants is to have a reputation as a toxic person. The hallmark of these toxic people is someone who sucks the energy out of others and causes tensions (not in a good way), acrimony and strife throughout their sphere of influence and, in general, creates havoc and chaos wherever they are. We all know people like this – they make your nightmares seem tame and make your anxiety rise whenever you interact with them. And the worse ones don't even know they are doing it. So imagine this person as your leader – the one leading you into battle, being the one person all others answer to, being the one that is in charge.

So what makes for an awful leader?

By understanding how the toxic leader behaves and acts you will understand what not to do and how the Real Estate Warrior employs techniques and actions to avoid such a state. Right off the bat the toxic leader lacks the ability to LISTEN. Listening to someone implies respect for that person's opinions and a willingness to receive their ideas and opinions in a meaningful way. Everyone wants to be heard – even if the leader disagrees with the other person's opinions it is important when building positive long lasting relationships that the opportunity to listen is taken by the leader. The toxic leader doesn't listen, doesn't value others or their opinions and maintains a "fishbowl" view in all situations. This dismissing action causes resentments and devalues each person in the relationship.

Toxic leaders like SECRECY. Keeping secrets is a favorite strategy of the toxic leader. When building positive long lasting relationships the ideal of transparency plays an important part. The more that I understand the "why" of your actions the more I can trust your opinion and ideas. Having a lack of transparency creates barriers and obstacles to gaining, maintaining and strengthening trust in relationships. The toxic leader plays everything "close to the vest", fails to inform followers of what the situation is and what actions are going to be taken. Without transparency there can be no trust and without trust there will not be positive, long lasting relationships.

Toxic leaders will not, cannot and refuse to let go of their ego. What is ego – according to psychology your ego is that thing that defines "one's own sense of self worth"[9]. Wait? What?

In other words, your ego is what you think of yourself, which means we all have an ego; some are just more inflated than others. Toxic leadership and inflated ego goes hand in hand with each other. Ever known someone who thinks they are "special" and that they seem to believe they are better than everyone. That person who has an exaggerated sense about themselves. They are not very hard to spot. There are times in which toxic leaders didn't necessarily start out as toxic but, through success, became toxic. In those situations the ego grew and grew out of control.

A particular type of dangerous combination is ego and narcissistic traits, which present a rather ugly display of leadership. This toxic leader not only has an inflated self image but has delusions of grandeur about all aspects of their life. When ask, everything is always "perfect" and life seems to be one special moment after another. Everything they do they believe they are the best at, they have the best car (regardless of make/model), the best business, the best family, etc…Unfortunately the "best" only involves the leader and does not apply to anyone else around them. These leaders initially look dynamic and attractive but the shine quickly disappears, leaving followers to search for more positive long lasting relationships elsewhere.

The ability to have EMPATHY, that quality that allows you to see things from another's point of view, is completely absent in the toxic leader. Because of the self-centeredness and the inflated sense of self-worth the toxic leader has the inability to recognize situations from any other point of view other than their own. As a leader one of your primary functions is to assist those you lead. The ability and function of leadership is to understand those barriers to success and get rid of them so everyone succeeds. The leader provides the resources to "get the job done".

The toxic leader does not because they cannot do this. Having empathy helps leaders provide the tools for those followers to succeed. The lack of empathy in the leader impacts on the culture of the organization in a dramatic fashion. Any real estate brokerage needs to function with a strong leader who provides resources, direction and a culture of success if there is to be positive, long lasting relationships. Organizations with toxic leadership may show success in the statistics and numbers (e.g. the number of transactions, total sales volume, etc) - year after year but have agents and staff constantly changing when they exit for more supportive organizational cultures.

In these situations there is typically a few sycophants that remain with the organization while the leader or leaders of the organization continue to be oblivious to the reasons for the turnover (hint: it's them, the leaders) and because they fail to recognize their own weaknesses they fail to make any positive changes.

Speaking of change – most toxic leaders are measureable failures at adapting to CHANGE. This inability to adapt is directly in relationship to leadership arrogance. One thing is constant in this world and that is things change. For the toxic leader change does not really apply. They are content in staying in their kingdom that they have built and believe that they will always win while others lose. This approach does not lend toward a culture of agent development, leadership development, and festers with poor communication and inconsistent messages to the followers.

WOW!!! Let's take a quick break and try to wash away all this negativity. At this point you are probably feeling like you could use a shower, wash off the negative leadership traits and look for something positive out of all this. I could not agree more.

These toxic leadership situations drains you intellectually, emotionally and physically, and makes you feel uninspired, and unappreciated and undervalued. The Real Estate Warrior understands this and works to avoid situations that leads to toxic leadership and by doing so is able to build positive long lasting relationships that thrive and lift everyone – we all succeed together!!!

WE ALL SUCCEED TOGETHER!!!

So let's crank up the positivity and begin re-charging our batteries as we explore the idea of Transactional Leadership. Remember we said leaders do the right thing and managers do things right. Transactional Leadership is about management and the ability and willingness for managing real estate transactions the "right way". In today's fast paced, instant gratification and get it now world the speed of a real estate transaction can be a challenge to many involved. The ability to manage the transaction and manage it in a positive manner that creates trust and understanding with those involved (remember all those people we listed in the last chapter) to bring about a smooth transaction and successful ending is key to the Real Estate Warrior's ability to succeed.

One of the most important aspects to any real estate transaction is having order and structure. The structure comes from the legal documents (e.g. agreement of sale) which outlines the terms of the deal – the closing date, what type of inspections and the time frame to complete them, the type of mortgage and when mortgage commitment is due, etc.

The Real Estate Warrior maintains this structure in every transaction and understands that order leads to effective communication with your client and builds trust. Real estate transactions require communication with a myriad of people and that process must move along in an organized manner. Being a Real Estate Warrior means having the ability to address the needs of your client throughout this organized process in a systematic fashion that keeps the timeline of events from getting off track. The key is managing individual performance while facilitating the entire group's performance.

So how does the Real Estate Warrior know when to be a transformational leader and when to be a transactional leader? The difference between the two types of leadership is key in understanding how the Real Estate Warrior knows when to use which type at the right time.

TRANSFORMATIONAL LEADSHIP IS ABOUT "SELLING" & TRANSACTIONAL LEADERSHIP IS ABOUT "TELLING"

Simply put the Real Estate Warrior will be a transformational leader during the "selling" part of a real estate relationship. At the beginning when converting leads into prospective buyers and sellers. When meeting with the client for the first time, getting to understand their needs and wants, and projecting confidence as their Real Estate Warrior are all part of the transformational leadership traits and actions to apply. Being likable, and being motivational and inspiring to your clients. Building that positive long lasting relationship from the first phone call, text or email is the first step and requires the Real Estate Warrior to be a transformational leader.

As the relationship progresses and clients begin to narrow their focus on the home that meets their needs and wants the Real Estate Warrior will have also developed a positive relationship with the client and will have built trust – trust that allows the client to have a high level of belief in you, their Real Estate Warrior and leads to the belief that you are looking after their best interest. The client also has a faith and trust in the abilities and knowledge that their Warrior is prepared to lead them into an offer (for buyers) or present an offer (for sellers) and is prepared to negotiate in their best interest.

Once the client is ready, willing and able to make the offer and have an offer accepted the Real Estate Warrior now must transition to being a transactional leader. The transactional leader emerges from the negotiations ready to bring and maintain order and structure, including keeping client's emotions (positive and negative) in check so that the transaction can move along to its successful conclusion. The Real Estate Warrior will feature positive reinforcement and appeal to the self-interest of the client while maintaining a priority for the group, as a whole, to progress toward the closing date for the transaction.

So we ask ourselves – What is the skill set a person needs to possess in order to manage these types of leadership roles and partake in actions and discussions that reflect the right kind of leadership at any given time? Most people will do things if there is a consequence or a reward attached to the behavior. The ability to recognize both the short term impact and long term affect all of our actions and words have is what makes a successful Real Estate Warrior.

Chapter 7
The Smart Working Warrior

Don't work harder – work smarter!!!

A phrase coined in the 1930's by Allan F. Mogensen, the creator of Work Simplification[10]. The Real Estate Warrior understands this concept and applies it to their practice every day. What exactly does it mean though? How in the world do I work smarter – and how do I know I'm even doing it?

The Real Estate Warrior, first and foremost, has a plan of attack. That plan is vital to success and maps out the "why's", the "how's" and the "what's" so that every person on the Warrior Team understands their role and how their role contributes to the success of the team. The plan has several components, each one just as important as the next and must be developed in a collaborative and knowledgeable manner AND must be a "breathing, living document" that is utilized every single day and can be adapted and adjusted as the market changes.

The components of the Warrior Plan are focused on being productive and do not confuse activity with accomplishment. The idea is straight forward – we all have 24 hours in a day and what we do with each of those hours becomes vital to our success. Now, in real estate, it is often said that there is no such thing as a "typical day". The Real Estate Warrior uses this as an advantage.

The components that will help the Real Estate Warrior to work smarter include:

Component #1 – Have Productive Habits
Component #2 – Know Your Day
Component #3 – Technology as a Tool
Component #4 – Your Time Your Money

Component #5 – Communication

Component #1 – Have Productive Habits

Working in real estate affords you the ability to be your own boss while also being part of a team (or Brokerage). The first step in being productive is knowing where your time goes. Starting and keeping an account of your time each day can help you understand how you use your time. This takes discipline and a willingness to look at ALL aspects of your business – the good, the bad and the ugly – and have a willingness to make changes to become more productive. The ultimate goal is to minimize interruptions and distractions that take away from productive activities that lead to positive results.

Is multi-tasking necessary to have productive work habits? Multi-tasking is the ability to "execute more than one task at the same time". Parents of toddlers understand this concept better than most people. The ***ability*** is the key to whether or not multi-tasking helps or hurts productivity. What is this "ability" and how do you know if you have it?"

This ability has to do with how quickly your brain recovers from its innate "start/stop process". Dr. Nancy K Naiper, PhD, of Boise State University has studied multi-tasking and believes that what most people are doing is "switch tasking", going from one task to another with this start/stop process in the brain and that in most cases, actually slows down the activity of the person[11]. By tracking your time and activities you can determine if multi-tasking should be part of your day.

Finally, when tracking your time and activities you will come to learn when you are most productive. Some folks do the majority of their work early morning and by afternoon tend to shut down, or they barely function in the a.m. but really are able to be productive into the afternoon and evening. By seeing in front of you on paper (or an App) how you structure your day AND what is achieved will help you move toward that ultimate goal of productive activities that lead to positive results. This is the first component of the Real Estate Warriors Plan for success, one that leads to knowing your day.

Component #2 – Know Your Day

Know my day? What the hell does that mean? Most of the time if a real estate agent can tell you what day of the week it is we are functioning ok. Real estate is a funny business – it doesn't have a set time line for activities and deals – a deal can happen at any time!!! For the Real Estate Warrior this understanding is the foundation of the "know your day" concept. When a buyer is ready to buy that's when they will make an offer. When a seller is ready to sell that's when they will put their home on the market. As a Real Estate Warrior you must be ready when your client is ready.

Let's talk about buyers – having a "ready, willing and able" buyer is the goal of every real estate agent. This means the buyer is pre-qualified for a mortgage or has presented proof of funds for a cash deal; that the buyer is a willing and a volunteer participant in a transaction and has not been coerced and has the legal ability to partake in a real estate transaction including being party to a legally binding contract. But that's just the tip of the iceberg, the bare minimum requirements for an offer to be made. Notice this is just the offer to purchase a home; we still don't have a legally binding agreement. Remember the goal is a legally binding agreement that results in the sale of a property. So, the agent is excited that an offer is being made. How did the agent get here? Knowing the signs that a buyer is ready to buy can help agents build trusting relationships while helping buyers feel more confident and secure.

You have been working with a client and have shown them several homes with no offers. The client states that the house isn't for them or "it's not the one". The Real Estate Warrior recognizes the emotional buyer and spends a great deal of time getting to know the home that will give the buyer a "feeling of home". It is this feeling the Real Estate Warrior is focused on when sending the buyer homes to look at. Typically once the buyer's feeling has been met the buyer may not want to leave the home and will spend time talking about where their belongings will go, how the kids will do their homework at the kitchen counter, and where the swing set will be in the yard. Once here, the buyer is ready to make the offer.

The buyer who has seen many homes and continues to reference a particular home that is used to compare all others. This comparison home needs to be revisited and discussed with the buyer. There is a reason the buyer keeps coming back to it.

When buying a home, the buyer is buying a used home!! Which means the buyer needs to understand that not everything about the home will be perfect. The buyer who accepts this concept becomes a buyer ready to make an offer.

Ok, now that you have an idea about buyers, let us look at those that wish to sell their home. The selling of a property can be a very emotional decision for some folks, for others it's a cold calculated business decision. The Real Estate Warrior needs to have a good understanding of the type of seller they are working with in order to have a positive relationship that can assist the seller in meeting their goal.

We can look at sellers and come to understand their motivation by discussing when a seller is NOT ready to sell their home. Market Testers are sellers who have priced their home well above the average for their location. These sellers aren't necessarily looking to sell their home or they have unrealistic expectations about the housing market in their area. Either way, a seller who is not interested in looking at a market analysis and reasonable home prices are not ready to sell their home. Not yet!!

Next you have the Chaos Households. These are homes that just cannot and will not stay ready to show. These are sellers that do not adhere to the 80/20 rule of de-clutter and de-personalization; meaning that the home should be cleared of 80% of all personal items (e.g. pictures, books, videos, flowers, etc...) that can distract a buyer from seeing the home. Instead, the sellers refuse to take down anything, refuse to put any items away and maintain the clutter and chaos that they are used to living in. Every time the home is shown the feedback is horrible and negative yet the sellers seem unphased.

Finally the Apathetic Seller – this is your seller who won't budge on the price, refuses to negotiate with a bona fide offer, takes the home off and puts it back on the market, or just plain drags out the selling process.

All these scenarios frustrate buyers and their agents, waste people's time and create situations that do not end well for anyone involved.

So as the Real Estate Warrior knowing your day is about knowing your buyers and sellers, where they are at in the buying / selling process and having a relationship that promotes productive activities each and every day.

Component #3 – Technology is a Tool

We are all aware of how technology has grown in the past 30 years. Technology game changers like the Internet have dominated the past three decades to the point that we make statements like "how did real estate ever get done before the Internet and email". The Real Estate Warrior understands that technology is an enhancement for and not a replacement of building positive, long lasting relationships with clients. As we discussed back in Chapter 3, the Real Estate Warrior will use technology to enhance the relationship and further build trust with clients. The speed of technology can bring about instant gratification for clients hungry for information about a particular home – especially if it is "the one" – and providing the client with said information sooner rather than later shows a respect for your client's needs and their time.

The use of technology keeps a record of events during a transaction so if there is ever a disagreement or dispute over something the transaction is "in writing" and all important decisions can be traced back to written (i.e. text messages, emails) correspondence.

Suffice to say, technology is an integral part to the home buying / selling process and will continue to evolve, allowing another advantage for the Real Estate Warrior.

Component #4 – Your Time Your Money

Time is the most valuable resource a real estate agent has. You can always make more money but you cannot make more time. What Ben Franklin was really talking about is opportunity costs. Opportunity costs simply defined are "a benefit that a person could have received, but gave up, to take another course of action"[12].

As a Real Estate Warrior where you devote your time determines how successful your business will be. The productivity value of your time is literally connected to the amount of money your business will make. Remember, real estate agents do not get paid for showing houses, for listing houses or for marketing their services....they get paid when they SELL A HOUSE!!! That's not to say those other activities are not important and are critical along the home buying / selling process, they are. But the end game and productivity numbers will be based in the number of properties that have been sold and the amount of commission collected.

Component #5 – Communication

Communication is the final component to the Real Estate Warriors plan of action. More importantly is effective and consistent communication with clients, other real estate agents, team members, Brokers, lenders, inspectors, appraisers, municipalities, insurance agents, and anyone else who is part of a real estate transaction. Remember that list of people involved in the real estate transaction?

Real Estate Transaction Team – Buyer, Buyer Agent, Buyer Closing Agent, Seller, Seller Agent, Seller Closing

Agent, Lender, Underwriter, Appraiser, Home Inspector, Municipalities, Insurance Agent, Movers

The Real Estate Warrior understands the importance of clear and concise communication with the real estate transaction team members – whether that be through telephone, email, snail mail, text message or pony express – the key to a successful transaction is communication.

The first thing to recognize is the *purpose of communication.* Communication in its simplest form is the exchange of information that leads to a shared understanding between the sender and receiver of the communication[13]. In other words, if I tell you something I want to make sure that you (1) understand what it is I said and (2) that you either agree or disagree with the information I have presented to you. Seems pretty straight forward – how could anything go wrong?

Communication or more to the point, the lack of communication has caused more trouble in real estate and real estate transactions than anything else. The Real Estate Warrior understands that the method and manner in which communication is accomplished can be the difference between a successful transaction and a forgettable transaction. Whether you are working with buyers or sellers it is important to always be mindful of the fact that the way you communicate with clients either builds trust or it doesn't.

Clients that want to believe their agent is "the best" – the best knowledge keeper, the best information giver, and the best negotiator – simply the best REALTOR!!! We are either building a positive long lasting relationship based on trust and mutual benefit or we are not. Our style of communication plays a huge role in how successful we can be in the real estate game.

The Real Estate Warrior understands that effective communication involves listening to your clients, hearing what they are asking and meeting their needs, having the ability to be concise and to the point with clients and developing the best method of communication with them. It's important that clients hear about your experiences and have them understand that you have "been there, done that". Maintaining positive body language and making eye contact all go a long way in establishing and building trust. For the Real Estate Warrior the most important aspect of communication is to be "present" with every client you are communicating with – meaning you are fully engaged with the client and do not allow distraction to reduce the quality of your time you are giving to your client. Treating every client as if they are the most important client you have – because they are!!!

Working smarter, not harder can be achieved and will bring about a return on investment of your time and relationship building with clients. The ability to do this up-front work will pay huge dividends in the long run and make the Real Estate Warrior's business strong and secure now and into the future.

Chapter 8
After the Sale

The closing date has come and gone – the transaction is concluded – buyers bought the home and the sellers sold the home. Everyone is happy and getting back to normal life – life after the transaction. But what about the Real Estate Warrior – a job well done but is it "Mission Accomplished"?

The short answer to that question is "No" as the relationship has just entered a new phase and the Real Estate Warrior now must decide if a positive, long lasting relationship is going to continue or not. Also, the client will need to decide as well. So what does the Real Estate Warrior have to decide – how not to stalk this client now that they have purchased or sold the home? The transactional leadership role has concluded with the consummation of the deal. The Real Estate Warrior now must move back into the transformational leadership role and begin the process of keeping your name "in front of the client".

This phase of building the positive, long lasting relationship needs to be approached with the utmost care and consideration by the Real Estate Warrior. To the client, you have performed your duties and satisfied their self-interest at the current time. The heightened senses that come along with the purchasing or selling process are now subsided and the day-to-day routines are now settling in. It could be said the last thing any buyer or seller really want is to hear from their real estate agent and certainly they do not need to deal with a sales pitch.

The Real Estate Warrior knows when to proceed and when to back off. The key to this phase being successful is knowing what to say, how to say it, and how to deliver the message.

So what is the right message, the right delivery of that message and how often do you provide some type of contact with clients that have finished the transaction? Before the answer to these questions become apparent, let's take a moment to look back at how the relationship has been developed thus far, and why the process of relationship building is just as important as the next steps in this next phase:

Phases of Client Relationship Building

Phase 1   Introduction & Rapport Building
                Getting to Know Each Other
                Acknowledgement of Needs & Wants
                Goal Establishment
                Demonstration of Knowledge
                Transformational Leadership Skill Set

Phase 2   Negotiating & Trust Building
                Establish boundaries & Ground Rules
                Best Foot Forward – "Is this the Right Agent?"
                Demonstration of Meeting Needs & Wants
                Faith in Agent Ability
                Transformational Leadership Skill Set

Phase 3   Facilitation Phase
                Trust & Value Strengthened
                Buy the Home / Sell the Home Process
                Tactician with the Transaction Team
                Successful Completion of Transaction
                Transactional Leadership Skill Set

So the "why" of building the client relationship is evident – the more positive a relationship is; build on a foundation of mutual respect of needs and wants and strengthened through a process that creates, builds and maintains trust and faith, all leading to a desired outcome. So the beginning of Phase 4 of the relationship building process really started from the first contact with the client.

With this phase the groundwork for understanding the client's new values, lifestyle and goals for the future is important to the Real Estate Warrior. Has the client found their "forever home" or is this their "starter home", is their goal to be in another home in 3 years, 5 years or longer, does the client need to find another agent in another geographical area because they have been transfered for employment purposes, have they retired or looking to downsize in the near future? – all these and a thousand other questions answered will drive the Real Estate Warrior in knowing how to proceed. The goal always at this phase is to maintain the relationship for future consideration of meeting the client's needs and wants.

So, how can you be "of value" to your client once the transaction of purchasing and/or selling of a home has been concluded? As an agent the client does not need your expertise or knowledge anymore, they don't need your access to homes or buyers or sellers anymore, and they certainly do not need your time (and subsequently their time) anymore as well. Your value has been diminished and the relationship has now changed. This concept of "value" becomes extremely important at this phase of the relationship building process.

What constitutes "value"? Value can be viewed as your relative worth and importance to your client. The value assigned by the client has been developed based on the actions and communication that has taken place throughout the relationship building process. The need to recognize the value of the relationship will help to determine what happens to the relationship after the sale has been concluded.

Typically one of three relationships will develop after the sale or transaction has concluded. The Real Estate Warrior must be prepared to address each one successfully:

(1) *The Ended Relationship*

In this scenario the client has made the decision that the value of the relationship ended with the completion of the transaction. The client makes the decision that their needs and wants have been met and the relationship does not need to continue. Typically the client will "opt out" of future email correspondence, or does not acknowledge or return text, emails or phone calls.

Strategy: The Real Estate Warrior's response to this type of relationship needs to be handled delicately and with tact and patience. The client has made clear their intentions, however, the consideration of a need or want in the future has not been recognized by the client. The very first thing the Real Estate Warrior must decide – "Is this a relationship worth continuing?" By figuring out the pros and cons of pursuing this client the Real Estate Warrior can determine if their valuable resources should be devoted to this client. The importance of understanding your client's wants and needs becomes a critical part of the analysis of the relationship. Remember, even if this client no longer has a need for your services, they most likely have family members, friends or others that do. The approach is one of an indirect branding type of campaign. Your main goal is to keep your name in front of the client in a very subtle manner. If the determination is that the client will now become a lead generator then the approach taken will reflect the Real Estate Warrior's goals for this client. If it is determined that this client no longer holds value then a polite and professional thank you and "good luck" will suffice.

(2) *The Collaborative Relationship*

By definition a collaboration is when two or more persons work together to realize or achieve something successfully. Sound familiar? It is during the transaction phase that a collaborative relationship is typically built between the agent and the client. Each party working together to achieve a successful outcome – namely the successful conclusion of the transaction. In this scenario the relationship that was developed and cultivated during the transaction phase extends pasts the conclusion of the transaction.

Strategy: The Real Estate Warrior and the client will both recognize the extension of this collaborative relationship as well as how the relationship has changed because the needs and wants have now changed. This strategy may become extremely important when working with buyers who are investors of property. Working with investors, the Real Estate Warrior understands the primary goal for the investor is to make money – either through "flipping" a property or establishing monthly income through rental properties. This relationship becomes one that lasts and develops past the initial completion of the transaction. The client's value perception revolves around the agent's ability to re-list the property once alterations/improvements have been made or to attract tenants that can rent the properties/units that have been purchased. In either case the perception of value may have changed but the relationship can be cultivated and strengthened by helping the client meet and exceed their new goals. This relationship is about taking the needs of the client into account, being willing to listen and understand the "new needs and wants" and utilizes the skill set to offer opportunities for those needs/wants to be met. In this relationship providing solutions is key.

(3)   *The Future Relationship*

In this scenario the relationship is neither ended nor collaborative but there exists for a possible renewal of the relationship sometime in the future. This is the bulk of relationship scenarios that the Real Estate Warrior will experience. It's during this relationship that clients and agents are not actively engaged in a relationship but are both aware that they may have the opportunity to be involved with each other again.

Strategy: The Real Estate Warrior approaches these scenarios with an open mind and open heart. Understanding that the important factor is timing – when will the client actually need your skill set again? Will it be when the client is ready to sell their home? Will it be when the client has a family member or friend that is looking to buy and sell a property? The client and the Real Estate Warrior are aware that the relationship will continue at a future date. The priority for the Real Estate Warrior is timely and effective communication with their client. This communication can be direct or indirect. Direct communication as in a phone call, text message or email that is relevant to your client's needs and wants. Indirect communication through flyers, mailers, emails that provide knowledge building and information about the market, trends or something you believe the client will find interesting. When discussions take place the Real Estate Warrior will always be professional and polite while being open and honest about fulfilling the needs and wants of the relationship. Through open and honest communication the respect and trust will continue to build, thus demonstrating to the client that the Real Estate Warrior is not just interested in the client as another sale. This strategy and approach is the crux of repeat and referral business – treat it well and the Real Estate Warrior will be rewarded in the long run.

Chapter 9
The Future Is for the Warrior

What does the future hold for real estate and the Real Estate Warrior? Will technology overrun the real estate industry? Will real estate agents become obsolete? Will Blockchain technology and Artificial Intelligence (AI) eclipse and forever change the landscape of real estate transactions? Wait. What?

What the hell is Blockchain technology? Is there another recession on its way and if so, when will it hit? Housing bubble – what housing bubble? Today's real estate industry is tomorrow's opportunities and the Real Estate Warrior recognizes opportunities and plans to succeed now and in the future.

FAILING TO PLAN IS PLANNING TO FAIL

How will the Real Estate Warrior prepare for the future? There are five steps that the Real Estate Warrior must do in order to be prepared to take advantage of opportunities that present themselves as the real estate industry and markets change. Understanding the market conditions and anticipating change is key to success – much easier said than done!!!

The following steps have been devised to assist the Real Estate Warrior in planning for the future:

Step 1 – Understand Current Resources and Capabilities

The Real Estate Warrior is constantly taking inventory of the strengths and weaknesses that exist in their business model and business practices. Understanding the nuances of the why, how and what is successful and unsuccessful transactions is key to maintaining and growing your business.

IN ORDER TO THRIVE TOMORROW YOU MUST UNDERSTAND TODAY

Step 2 – Read, Read, Read and Then Read Some More

Understanding the industry you work in makes for competitive advantages over the agent who is trying to "time the market" and is praying for their next sale. There are multiple sources the Real Estate Warrior can draw from to gather research and information about the industry trends, statistics, and opinions. In fact, there is so much information that "paralysis by analysis" needs to be avoided. This can occur when there is too much information trying to be processed and understood by the individual that they are unable or unwilling to make a decision or move to action, causing them to stand still, which creates the unenviable situation of getting passed by the competition.

IN BUSINESS, AS IN LIFE, IT IS IMPORTANT TO KEEP MOVING FORWARD

Step 3 – Take Calculated Risks

Would you fly to Las Vegas, walk into a casino and plunk down oh say $10,000 on number 19 at a Roulette table? Would you plunk down $10? Which is more to your liking? It's an important answer for the Real Estate Warrior. In order to succeed you need to be willing to take some risks, and as they say the higher the risk the higher the reward.

Unfortunately, a lot of businesses (remember you are a real estate business not just a real estate agent) take far too many risks and end up failing to achieve their goals. Real estate is risky enough to be flying off half-cocked and hoping for the best. The

Real Estate Warrior understands the concept of calculated risk.

THE DIFFERENCE BETWEEN RISK AND CALCULATED RISK IS THE OUTCOME

For the Real Estate Warrior a calculated risk is an action that is measured and purposeful that is based on a probability of success or failure. There needs to be a tolerance threshold held by the Real Estate Warrior and the business and this threshold helps to determine if the action will be set in motion. But why take a risk at all?

Risk is something that invigorates us, makes us feel alive and keeps us from getting into a rut. The worst place for a business to be is in a rut. Doing the same thing over and over again and expecting different results is the definition of insanity according the Alcoholics Anonymous. The idea that taking risks is outside the norm or beyond the boundaries of a business or a business leader is almost laughable – considering that this country and our economy has been build, bred and transformed by risk takers. The Real Estate Warrior doesn't take risks but rather takes calculated risks!! The importance of understanding that how to balance logic and facts with emotions makes the calculated risks and associated returns worth it.

Step 4 – Always Be Evaluating

The Real Estate Warrior understands that numbers are extremely important and vital to gaining understanding and increasing knowledge of market conditions, your competition and the industry in general. The more you know the quicker you will act, react and move forward. The key to numbers is having the right ones and understanding what they mean. Every business should have some basic analytics and metrics in which to gauge the success or failure of the business model and plans being utilized. If this sentence confused you, you didn't understand it or can't "wrap your head around it", I would suggest stopping right now and signing up for a basic Business 101 course at your local college.

YOU CAN'T DEFINE WHAT YOU CAN'T COUNT BUT YOU CAN DESCRIBE IT

Evaluation is not limited to just numbers mind you. There is a whole science devoted to qualitative data research and analysis. The idea of qualitative data collection is designed to capture the description where quantitative data collection is designed to define. It is through this description that the Real Estate Warrior can more fully see the business model and practices while enriching their own understanding of its strengths and weaknesses. The ability to combine both description of and definition to the business model and processes creates the ability to see the whole picture.

So what kind of qualitative data collection can the Real Estate Warrior do? And how should it be done? In the social constructs that is our reality collecting the description instead of the definition is not as difficult as it may seem. You walk through your office and have a conversation with a few agents and the receptionist and find out that they all do not like the new office chairs or the phone system. You email a survey out to your clients asking for their opinion about your new buyer agent flyer. In both these activities you are collecting information that describes something and provides you with data that allows you to more fully understand "a something".

Step 5 – ABC – Always Be Closing

The Real Estate Warrior understands the importance of ABC. This is a mindset and an attitude that allows the Real Estate Warrior to look for opportunities to increase business, increase referral sources, increase leads and prospects, increase opportunities to list new homes, show more homes, make more offers and close more transactions – it is the core and essence of the Real Estate Warrior.

Now a point of clarification is needed – The Real Estate Warrior does not take the "Glengarry Glen Ross" approach to this sales mantra. In the movie Glengarry Glen Ross the ABC approach is one of cut throat, no holds bar, take it or have it taken from you. In other words, take the idea of a Zero Sum Game and put it into action by annihilating the other guy. While there does exist this mentality in agents and brokers to win at all costs it can be a dangerous approach that leads to short cuts, back room deals and a bending of ethics and rules to make the sale. **The Real Estate Warrior does not and will not condone such actions!!!**

IF YOU ARE NOT CLOSING SOMEONE ELSE IS

For the Real Estate Warrior the ability to always be closing is to view opportunities that exist every day in the market and industry. Through careful and targeted research and by conducting both external and internal evaluations of your business and the market you can make success happen. The ability to do this in a fair and ethical manner and being respectful of your clients, your colleagues and the industry itself, is the ABC of the Real Estate Warrior.

Knowing your client's needs and wants and having a solution to meet those needs and wants – whether it be the perfect 3 bedroom, 2 bath ranch sitting on 5 acres of land in a particular school district with low taxes for your buyer or that same home in which your seller is ready to sell – the key to ABC is knowing when the client is ready.

And Finally. . .

Now that you have learned the basics of being the Real Estate Warrior it is now time to put what you have learned into action. It is important to remember that real estate is about relationships and building positive long lasting relationships that are a mutual benefit to you and your client.

It is important to remember that being a Real Estate Warrior is about being successful in real estate through a well planned and executed business model. A plan that garners respect and trust that leads to repeat clients and referrals from well satisfied clients who respect your abilities and knowledge while providing top notch service.

It is important to remember that the real estate transaction involves a whole team of people who need and want leadership from the real estate agent and that your leadership will drive the transaction. Your leadership will create opportunities for success for everyone on the team and ultimately your leadership will bring the transaction to a successful conclusion... use it well.

Finally, the real estate industry, like all things, will change and morph into whatever it will become, the Real Estate Warrior is poised and ready to take on the new landscape and use the latest technologies to enhance (not replace) the expertise that all buyers and sellers will continually seek out ... be that Real Estate Warrior and I wish you much success now and in the future.

[Volume 1 Concluded]

Disclaimer

About the Author

First off thank you for purchasing and reading my book. It is my sincere hope that the writings have brought you a more effective understanding of leadership and being successful in real estate as well as in your life circumstances.

I have lived my life in Western Pennsylvania, residing in the small yet resilient town of Johnstown. I received my Bachelor's degree in Sociology from the University of Pittsburgh at Johnstown. I earned my Masters in Business Administration (MBA) and the designation of PhD (a.b.d.) [all but dissertation] from Indiana University of Pennsylvania. I have put that knowledge to use in leadership positions for over 25 years.

I have been happily married since 1991 and, along with my wife, Pam; have raised 2 boys and 5 dogs.

Notes

Chapter 1

1. *Page 9*   www.studentloanhero.com
2. *Page 10*   www.creditcard.com, LLC

Chapter 3

3. *Page 36*   www.dictionary.com

Chapter 4

4. *Page 39*   "My 200K Lesson: 3 Relationship-Building Tips for
             Agents". www.inman.com/2017/12/06
5. *Page 43*   "How to Create Clients for Life.
             https://blog.bufiniandcompany.com/create-clients-life/

Chapter 5

6. *Page 50*   https://www.nar.realtor/research-and-tatistics/quick-
             real-estate-statistics
7. *Page 51*   http://bea.gov/newsreleases/national/gdp/
             gdpnewsrelease.htm
8. *Page 52*   https://www.nar.realtor/research-and-tatistics/quick-
             real-estate-statistics

Chapter 6

9. *Page 68*   www.dictionary.com

Chapter 7

10. *Page 78* www.theleadershipnotebook/8-powerful-traits-of-
             effective-leaders/
11. *Page 81* "The Myth of Multitasking".
             https://www.psychologytoday.com/blog/creativity-
             without-borders-201405/the-myth-multitasking
12. *Page 89* http://www.businessdictionary.com/
             definition/opportunity-cost.html
13. *Page 91*   www.businessdictionary.com/
             definition/communication.htlm

www.ingramcontent.com/pod-product-compliance
Lightning Source LLC
Chambersburg PA
CBHW071325220526
45468CB00001B/497